A GORGEOUS, MESSY LIFE

Snapshots of Gratitude from a Global Yogi

ANNA FOLMER

Verlag: BoD · Books on Demand GmbH, Überseering 33, 22297 Hamburg, bod@bod.de
Druck: Libri Plureos GmbH, Friedensallee 273, 22763 Hamburg
ISBN (Print): 978-3-7597-7862-8

Photo credits: Cover photo, Peacock Pose, Revisited and Showing Up in New Ways photos courtesy of The Solebury Club, USA; A Failed Stretch Test photo by Robyn Graham, USA; The Cheering Friends and Gravity Sucks photos by Juffing Hotel & Spa, Austria
Cover and Book Design: Angelique Carmello, USA

To my family—Arindam, Linnea, Andreas, Nishant and Pawan—
for their daily inspiration, encouragement and love

CONTENTS

INTRODUCTION

My husband Arindam always says: "I am just so fortunate that I have gotten the opportunity and had the experience."

Opportunities, I have had.

I grew up in the Netherlands with a Swedish mom and a Frisian (coastal Netherlands) dad.

I spent twenty-five years in the United States on both coasts (Pennsylvania and California), where I met and married Arindam (from India), and had four kids.

We lived in Singapore for a few years. Now, we live in Austria. Linnea and Andreas, our oldest children, live in the Netherlands; Nishant and Pawan still live at home with us. Large family gatherings reflect four continents, seven nationalities, eight languages, and four religions.

Through decades of living worldwide, integrating into new communities and cultures, and raising kids, my yoga practice has both grounded and propelled me. I found yoga in 1998, became a certified instructor the next year, and have been teaching ever since.

I have taught yoga in local gyms, boutique studios, and hotels; under coconut trees, on the Autobahn, and with Afghan refugees in an Austrian alpine village. And like many practitioners, upon the pandemic of 2020, I started teaching yoga online.

This book is a selection of edited blogs that accompanied my weekly online classes from 2020-2024 and that resonated with my international audience. Some skipped the class, but stayed for the story.

The blogs reflect the reality of trying to lead a global life aligned with yogic teachings and values. Things get messy. I am not perfect.

But I am always filled with gratitude.

CHAPTER ONE

COMING TO YOGA

A FAILED STRETCH TEST

I gained yoga teaching accreditation when I was a young mother. Therefore, I assumed my kids would go through life with a regular yoga practice.

Never had I imagined that my kids would fail a stretch test.

Nishant failed his stretch test in a California middle school. And if we were still living there, my youngest, Pawan, would have failed it, too.

Austrian middle schools don't include stretches as part of fitness assessment; they test students' strength and speed.

But flexibility is tied to speed. So while Pawan didn't fail the fitness test, he wasn't the top in his class.

The fastest student was the one who could touch his toes. Pawan can barely touch his knees with straight legs. So he asked me to help with flexibility.

I showed Pawan a few stretches and we did them together several times. I wrote them down so Pawan could do them on his own. He told me he would do them every day, and the days he had soccer practice/games, he would try to do them twice.

I didn't keep my expectations high.

But when I walked into Pawan's room the other day to wish him goodnight, he was in a thigh stretch (with labored breathing and a clenched jaw).

My Yogi-Mom's dream came true!

Pawan is still stretching months later, but not regularly. He didn't see results fast enough.

I know that like all parental lessons, my son will come back to stretching or yoga when the time is right for him, not for me.

THIS HOUSE IS MY NEW YOGA

We started moving into our new house in a small Austrian alpine village. The heat is not working properly, so we are not living there yet.

It feels like this house is my new yoga practice.

Deep breaths aid my patience in awaiting the replacement of the one, tiny sensor in the solar panel system. Flexibility helps me adjust to every next hurdle that comes with moving into a new house. Physical strength allows safely lifting boxes and moving furniture. Mindfulness on the next right step in our renovation gives me faith that this project will be accomplished.

Like my yoga practice, I know our new home does not have to be perfect. But hopefully, it will become the same safe place that my yoga mat is.

My only concern is that after twenty-five years of yoga, I still cannot get into Hanumanasana (full split). Will this house also not be fully realized in twenty-five years?

NISHANT MOMENTS

I have invited my boys countless times to join me on my mat. I know that the practice offers physical and mental benefits, including for younger people and those difficult young-adult years.

But what teenager follows their parents' advice?

Nishant (seventeen years) thinks yoga is for old people. He doesn't think it's cool to hang out with me. He claims stretching hurts.

Andreas (twenty years) has consistently ignored his parents pleas to move, to bike, to go for a run, to do anything to counteract all the hunching over his computer while studying in college.

On the rare occasions they join me, it is all Drama.

A recent session with Nishant began with confidence in Cat/Cow stretches. But he started groaning in Downward Facing Dog. He thought his hamstring was going to tear when we moved to Standing Forward Fold. By the time we were in a low runner's stretch, Nishant asked me if a muscle could snap. He accused me of abuse during thigh stretches and of torture at core work.

He ran out when our half-hour session was up.

But at dinner that night, Nishant reported that his body was feeling "really good" and that maybe yoga wasn't so bad after all.

And today I got a text message from Andreas. I had to read it twice to believe my eyes:

"Hej, Mamma, I have started doing a few yoga stretches in the morning for my back to feel better. Maybe you can send me a few more yoga exercises?"

It was music to my ears!

I made him a 15-minute video he can do in the morning and at night.

We all have those Nishant/Andreas-like moments when we hesitate toward yoga, when poses feel too difficult, when the practice does not feel fun.

Yet our future self knows when we practice yoga now, we feel better later.

"What teenager follows their parents' advice? But our future self knows when we practice yoga now, we feel better later."

YOGA IS FOR EVERYBODY

When vacationing in Mexico, my friend, Milou, and I sought out a yoga class in a neighborhood studio. The studio looked open and felt good. It had a restaurant offering organic juices and sandwiches in the front. We were excited!

When we entered the studio, everyone stared. I thought it was because we were so clearly foreigners. When we inquired about classes, locals informed us that the ability level was high, the classes difficult and physically strenuous.

Milou and I felt discouraged and unwelcomed not because we were foreigners, but because we were twice as old as the average student.

Naturally, our first instinct was to sign up for the hardest class to show the group we could keep up.

But then maturity kicked in, and we decided that yoga on the beach was a better way to spend our time.

When I'm teaching, I love to see college students next to Golden Years students taking yoga together. When we mix ages, backgrounds, and abilities, we bolster the richness of a class and of our lives.

ONCE A YOGI, ALWAYS A YOGI

We spent a few days in Bilbao, Spain, with our boys and a few friends.

We walked around the city, talked, ate good food and drank good Rioja. We swam and the boys surfed.

We hadn't surfed in the five years since we had lived in California, so I was curious to see if the boys had forgotten how. But they popped up as if it was just yesterday that they had last surfed. (Although, the boys were quite sore in the evening.)

Yoga is like surfing; the body remembers.

— CHAPTER TWO —

COMMUNITY

PENNSYLVANIANS CHECK ON THE SWEDES

We returned from hosting our annual yoga retreat. Andreas and his friends were around for Oktoberfest. Arindam welcomed all of us with a home-cooked Indian dinner, which he served to yogis and visiting Oktoberfest party-going young men alike.

Now that our guests have left, I am taking time to reflect on the retreat. As always, we had stunning views, cooling swims, beautiful food like crisp bread, and fun yoga sessions.

It is the connection with people at these retreats that means the most to me: laughter, friendship, and acceptance of each other. There is a feeling of belonging that I always find in any yoga setting.

I feel that sense of a community through our international online yoga classes.

Since May 2020, we have practiced together with friends, pets, and (Grand)kids. We have shared hard times when dear ones passed away, others got sick, quite a few had surgery, and lockdown wore us down.

I like that when I join the class, some of you are already chatting and catching up. I like that when the Swedes have not been around for a while, the Pennsylvanians will check in to see if everything is alright.

It warms my heart.

"It is the connection with people at these retreats that means the most to me: laughter, friendship, and acceptance of each other."

Susanne's Yoga Retreat Crisp Bread
Chef and co-owner of Hotel Du Soleil in Saint Raphaël

INGREDIENTS:

180 grams (6⅓ oz) corn flour
180 grams (6⅓ oz) mixed seeds (sunflower, flax [brown and yellow], sesame seeds etc.)
2 tablespoons olive oil
1 teaspoon salt
A little more than 230 grams (8 oz) water

1. *Mix all ingredients in a bowl by hand or heavy electric mixer (such as KitchenAid®).*
2. *Roll out between two greaseproof papers. Roll thinly.*
3. *Bake at 180°C (360°F) for 10-15 minutes.*

TIME FOR COFFEE

The chimney sweep helped me adjust to our small village's local customs and regulations.

The chimney sweep, or the Kaminkehrer, comes three times a year to clean the chimney and to verify that it is working well. This is mandatory.

I was surprised the first time our chimney sweep showed up. I hadn't known what a Kaminkehrer was and I had not requested him. He patiently explained everything to me in a mix of German and gestures.

The second or the third time the Kaminkehrer came, he told me he had some time for a coffee.

Again, I was surprised.

Soon, I realized that in our Austrian alpine village, when a person comes to your house for a job, the custom is to offer them coffee.

Now, the Kaminkehrer and I share a cup of coffee three times a year. I have coffee with the guy who fills the oil tank, with the Internet techie who is updating our Wi-Fi, the electrician who is fixing a light, the plumber, and anyone else who comes to the house to help maintain it.

They visit for about twenty minutes: When they don't understand my accent, it tends to be shorter, but when my son is at home speaking in dialect about soccer, they stay longer. Recently, two repair men saw our son's trumpet in the living room, picked it up, and started playing (while I was making the coffee).

Adjusting to coffee with the fix-it person is like the ongoing adjustment in my yoga practice. I see a teaching or a pose in a new light as I dig into my practice a little deeper, just as I do as I get to know more about the people who help us make our home the safe, warm place we want it to be.

Great-Grandmom Lagergren's Swedish Cake For Coffee

INGREDIENTS:

3 eggs
A little less than 2 dl (1 cup) of sugar
200 grams (7 oz) melted butter
2.25 dl (1 cup) flour
Raspberry jam (Sylt)

1. *Whisk the eggs and sugar well. Stir in the melted butter and flour.*
2. *Divide batter over three round baking forms to bake 3 three thin cakes. If it is not a springform cover, line inside of baking dish with baking paper. Bake in 200°C (390°F) pre-heated oven for about 12 minutes.*
3. *Let it cool slightly.*
4. *Take one round cake, spread raspberry jam on it, cover with second cake, add jam and cover with the third cake.*
5. *Cut the cake in strips diagonally across and again from the other directions to make rhombus-shaped little cakes.*

"When I dig a little deeper, I see a teaching or a pose in a new light; just as I do when I get to know the people who help make our home the safe, warm place we want it to be."

CHEERING FRIENDS

I teach yoga classes daily at the Juffing Hotel & Spa in Hinterthiersee.

Recently, a group of friends joined us. Some were experienced yogis, others were newbies.

One of the beginners nailed Crow pose on her first try. This is not an easy feat. The cheering that went on in that room could be heard outside!

It was a beautiful experience—not because this newbie accomplished the pose—but because of the true pleasure it gave others to see their friend succeed.

SISTER BLESSINGS

My favorite Bengali ceremony is a sibling ceremony called bhai phota. The sister blesses her brother(s) and wishes them a long and prosperous life. The date of this celebration is determined by the Hindu lunar calendar, but it usually falls around the end of October or early November.

This was an easy ceremony to celebrate when all the kids lived at home, but it's not so easy since Linnea moved away.

But last weekend, we were all in Amsterdam to celebrate Linnea's Master's degree graduation, so we added bhai phota to our schedule. Linnea blessed her brothers, which benefits her: Brothers are supposed to take care of their sisters for the rest of their lives.

Our kids treat each other like most other siblings do. They alternately fight and get along, yet always look out for each other. Even during the ceremony, the siblings were making fun of one another. But also, there was laughter and ganging up against parents, just as it should be.

Siblings are special. Friends may come and go, but siblings are forever.

If you are fortunate enough to have a sibling, send them a prayer, a card, or a call to let them know how special they are to you.

BOLLYWOOD IS UNIVERSAL

A few months ago, I began volunteering with a refugee agency that helps those from Afghanistan, Syria, Turkey, and elsewhere.

I was paired up with a young man from Afghanistan, Khalil, because I teach yoga and he is experienced in meditation. After a couple of hikes and a few cups of tea, we decided to teach yoga and meditation at the refugee center where he lives.

The class was so successful that the agency asked us to teach in Kufstein, where they have a larger refugee center to hold events.

Khalil and I opened the next class to Austrian locals, expats (mostly from Greece and Latvia) and refugees alike. Our hope was that bringing together people through yoga and meditation would help build community.

Not everyone here is happy about having refugees living in town; there are stereotypes and anxieties about them. But the better we know each other, the fewer stereotypes we have about each other, the less there is "other" and "them."

All of us have had to correct stereotyping. When I was young and traveling, people often asked me if I carried marijuana when they heard I was Dutch. When Linnea traveled to China during her American high school days, her host dad was disappointed when he learned that we did not own a gun. He had assumed all Americans carried them.

Khalil and I hoped to mitigate some stereotypes to ease locals and refugees living among each other.

I didn't know if anyone would show up. My neighbors said that they might come and I "requested" Arindam to join. From Khalil's home, seven refugees said they would attend.

But when it was time to leave for the class, all the refugees who had signed up backed out. I was bummed. And I was embarrassed to admit to Arindam and my neighbors that I couldn't pull off something like this.

Yet as we were waiting for the arrival of the social worker who helps facilitate our classes, two cars pulled in with my neighbor's friend and one of my regular students from Greece.

Then a commotion started in and around the refugee center. We saw windows open with people sticking out their heads, curious to find out what was going on. We heard cheering and shouting in various languages, and people laughing. A few refugees trickled into the yoga room. Following that, some cars pulled in and locals got out with their yoga mats in hand.

Ultimately, we had twenty-five students, a sound mix of fifteen refugees, some expats, and locals. In fact, there were so many that we ran out of yoga mats and of ways to translate for all who were there.

We taught in German, and those who didn't understand the language tried to copy the poses from sight. We performed partner poses, cheered each other on in difficult poses, and laughed when someone grunted. Grunting in a yoga pose needs no translation!

After class, locals and refugees asked when we were going to do this again. We plan on monthly classes to continue community connections.

And I plan on continuing to bring Arindam. Every refugee he spoke with asked about Bollywood when they realized he was Indian. Turns out that Hindi movies are the perfect common icebreaker.

"The better we know each other, the fewer stereotypes we have about each other, the less there is "other" and "them." "

— CHAPTER THREE —

PERSISTENCE

GRAVITY SUCKS

Recently, I watched a young child try to stand up and take their first steps. It brought me back to the days when my own kids were learning to walk.

Our children would fall countless times, day in and day out, month after month. We were thinking of getting them T-shirts that read, "Gravity Sucks."

But they never gave up. They didn't get frustrated or even tired of trying. And they did it with a smile. What an unbelievable amount of persistence and determination!

We lose some of that persistence as we age. Have we learned that when we get knocked down, it's hard to get up? Do we shy away from Difficult because like water, we are always flowing in the direction of least resistance?

Let's keep the persistence of that little-kid mentality when we practice, add an element of play, especially when we cannot find our balance. Instead of frowning, smile and think, "Gravity Sucks!"

And try again. It might help you off the mat the next time you stumble.

"Have we learned that when we get knocked down, it's hard to get up?"

THE IKEA® CLOSET

We bought Nishant an IKEA® closet for his room in the new house and began to build it as soon as we came home. We were excited to complete his room and especially, to move his boxes of clothes out of the basement.

But soon after we started, we stopped for dinner. Then Nishant went to his weekend job. We halted the closet work.

The next day, we just *had* to go skiing, so the closet remained half-finished. At night, Nishant put together the drawers, but then it was time for bed.

Then came Monday, and with it came school, homework, the gym, a nap, a shower... anything that seemed more important than completing this closet. Meanwhile, we were maneuvering ourselves around belongings (a desk, a surfboard, etc.) that were temporarily moved into the hallway to make room for the closet work.

It took us a week to finish the closet.

As I was observing this process, I couldn't help but smile. It reflected how I approach enhancing my asana practice.

I decide to work a little harder to master a pose or to become more flexible, especially in my hip flexors and quadriceps. At first, I'm excited. I make a plan and commit myself to one hour of yoga working on the particulars of what I want to improve.

After a week, I start finding excuses not to practice. Or if I do practice, the practice reflects more of the poses I like.

But to achieve anything new, whether that be a new pose or a new skill or a new habit, we need to be persistent, to have patience, and to have trust in the process. These are talents I lack in growing my own practice, but offer in abundance as a teacher in guiding and continually encouraging my students.

So I signed up for a friend's yoga intensive course. She loves poses I don't, she is strict, and she has patience. And she is incredibly committed.

"To achieve anything new, whether that be a new pose or a new skill or a new habit, we need to be persistent, to have patience, and to have trust in the process."

EGGS AT THE TOP OF THE ALM

Good friends invited us to go for a hike to Waller Alm, a place we had not yet visited. At the top of any mountain in Tirol there is a restaurant, an Alm.

We accepted the invitation, although we had no idea how difficult the hike would be. We tend to say Yes! as much as we can, then adapt on the fly.

The hike began with a steep uphill climb.

As we continued to ascend, Arindam started asking our friend, a biologist, more questions about the different mushrooms. I think he was stalling for a break instead of directly asking for one. And I secretly hoped he would keep asking until we got to the top.

(I recall my Pennsylvania yoga students at Flip Dog and Dig Yoga and The Solebury Club in Bucks County using the same technique, asking for yet another demonstration….)

After climbing 122 floors and walking 10.4 km (6.5 miles), we reached the Alm. I don't think I ever had eggs that tasted as good as they did in that moment.

"After climbing 122 floors and walking 10.4 km (6.5 miles), we reached the Alm. I don't think I ever had eggs that tasted as good as they did in that moment."

PEACOCK POSE, REVISITED

I started taking German classes again.

We have had a private tutor, Anita, since we arrived in Austria. But she worked mostly with the boys to help them pass German exams.

My German isn't bad, but it could be improved. And I have promised the many repeat Juffing hotel guests that I will teach Savasana in German within seven months, by year's end. Repeat guests and I joke that next time they come back, they will be able touch their toes and I will be able to speak perfect German.

Speaking German is one thing. But sounding relaxed while instructing Relax using synonyms as I know them in English ("soften," "let go of all your tension") is wholly different.

It took Anita and I more than two hours to develop "relaxation" text in German. I haven't yet told her that I also promised guests that my next goal is to speak grammatically correct German by the end of 2024.

I won't be devastated if I don't reach my goal. Speaking grammatically correct German is difficult, particularly when the locals speak mostly in dialect.

But I do enjoy setting small, manageable goals. And even after twenty-five years of practice, I still have yoga goals.

I came across this picture of Peacock pose and I want to see if I can still get into it.

I don't recall when I did it last.

DREAM COME TRUE

Years ago, a friend and I were sharing a cup of tea when she asked me to define my dream job.

I hadn't given it much thought. The children were young and I was up to my neck in diapers, laundry, volunteering in school, playdates, and all other things Motherhood. Who could think about anything beyond the day-to-day?

Upon reflection, I said that I would like to have a place where people come together to recharge, make friends, and bond over similar passions. I pictured an old farm with a yoga and art studio. I envisioned a giant table in the yard where meals could be shared. I would run the yoga classes and great artists would be invited to guide and explore different ways to create.

A decade later, I am hosting this yoga and art retreat with my friend, Leah.

We don't have a beautiful farm, nor an art or yoga studio.

But we will explore art and yoga in June in the beautiful alpine surroundings. Likely, we will make new friendships and bond over our common interests.

And we have a large table where meals will be shared and dreams such as mine are realized.

— CHAPTER FOUR —

ADVERSITY

EFFORT AND EASE

In yoga as in life, we must find a balance between effort and ease.

Strength, hard work, persistence, and solidity all are needed to grow in a yoga practice, to excel at work, to raise children, and to meet all of life's challenges.

But an equal amount of flexibility, softness, pliability, and letting go also is required to thrive.

Envision a tree: Its solid base and deep roots keep it strong so that it can remain steady as it sways in the wind. Too strong and the wind will snap its branches. Too flexible and the wind will topple the tree. It needs both to survive a storm.

I love poses that require strength (think handstands and plank). But I am not flexible, so I don't like poses such as splits or double pigeon.

Yet to maintain balance, we need the poses we shy away from as much or more than those poses into which our bodies simply flow.

If we lean into only Easy in our bodies or in our lives, we won't grow.

"In yoga as in life, we must find a balance between effort and ease. If we lean into only Easy, we won't grow."

A BLAEDE NUDEL

The meanest person I have ever come across in my life came back to the Juffing hotel.

The last time this woman was here, she approached me after class and lectured me for ten minutes about how terrible my German was. My German was so awful that it "hurts one's ears to listen to me."

The woman recommended I tape myself speaking to confirm how horrible I sound. She advised me to listen to someone speaking "good German" and to copy it until I sounded the same.

I was close to tears as I drove home. (I might have wiped my eyes, but am too proud to admit that.)

If I took out the emotion and purely listened to the message, she was right. I am still developing fluent and dialect German.

But her message delivery was hurtful. My boss called this lady a "Blaede Nudel" a Tyrolian expression.

Thankfully, hotel guests leave after a short stay.

But the woman was back in class again this week.

As soon as I realized it, my shoulders tightened, my breath shallowed, and my focus narrowed to her.

I tried to ignore the woman, but found that impossible when she closed the door in someone's face who was five seconds late. I ended class with a meditation about sending love and well-being to others.

I pondered on the drive home about calling in Sick the next day. But then this lady would "win."

We discussed my dilemma over dinner. Arindam said to ignore her. Nishant told me to "fight fire with fire." I said that we all have a backstory and unknown challenges that call for kindness.

The next day, I wore my "Love Is an Action Word" sweater and I planned another kindness meditation. When I arrived at work, I found that she had already left.

But I know she will be back.

KICKING BUTT WITH ONE LEG

Last Saturday, we went skiing and had a great time.

But during my last run, I had a small fall. No big tumble, not from jumping, just one of those little falls.

Normally, I would get up and continue. Not this time. I couldn't stand on my leg and I had heard a small crack.

I am now in the hospital (during the pandemic) with a steel plate and screws in my leg. I will be here for at least one more week, sharing a room with two ninety-year-olds who have broken hips plus a Centenarian. I am practicing my German with them.

There are at least 2,000 yoga poses, so we can find enough poses to fill an hour that don't include legs. Or I can talk you through poses. I can still kick butt with one leg!

A DIFFERENT RELATIONSHIP TO GRAVITY

It has been five weeks since I broke my leg.

I am back to teaching and slowly integrating practice with my classes. I still cannot put weight on my leg, but I can do all seated poses and most reclined poses.

There are surprisingly so many poses that do not exert weight on the legs. My dear friend and fellow yoga teacher at The Solebury Club in Bucks County, PA, Karin Eisen of KEYoga, says that there are only twelve basic poses. Recreating those shapes in different relationships to gravity form the roughly 2,000 yoga poses.

I feel physically and mentally so much better since I started to move my body again. A full body stretch and a twist can change the outlook of the day. I have flipped my broken-leg mentality to being grateful for my "normal" body parts and all I can do.

The ability to assess any situation from different angles helps me move through it.

RESTAURANT

NO SUGARCOATING BREAKS BARRIERS

I tend to be straightforward in instruction, more Dutch (and German) than the American's effusiveness I admire. American students from Optimal Fitness in Pennsylvania to Sweat Sanctuary in California used to comment on my frankness.

I got a taste of my own medicine at the doctor's office.

I went for a check-up, lymph drainage, and physical therapy. When I walked into the office on my crutches, my physician blurted, "Oh my, you look horrible, your walk is terrible!"

I expected, "Hello, nice to see you."

The doctor instructed me how to walk. I needed to put my heel down (no weight) and lift my toes higher. When I said that I couldn't lift them higher, he pushed back: "Yes, you can."

The doctor called the physical therapist to inform him that my walk was terrible and he needed to work on it "starting ASAP."

After I recovered from the shock of my physician's candidness, I realized my doctor truly wanted me to walk again without any limp or discomfort as soon as possible. He was not sugarcoating in my best interest.

Is directness a good way to help people break through barriers?

This was always my goal with it in teaching. I want my students to grow and to be protected from injuries. I never realized my honesty could be taken in a negative way given pure intentions.

At the end of the doctor's visit, I told my physician that my goal was to walk up one of the mountains in September and to eat lunch at the restaurant at the Alm.

He said he would do anything in his power to get me there.

I aim for the same goal with my students.

A COMPLETE LOSS OF WORDS

My English is quite okay and my German is coming along. I am fluent in Dutch and Swedish.

But I am at a complete loss of the right words to express myself in any language about recent events in our household.

Pawan, Nishant, and I went skiing on the 31st of December. It was icy, but it was nice to get out into some fresh air. And we are accomplished skiers.

Pawan found this little jump, something he routinely does. But just before he jumped, his ski hit ice and fell off. He consequently landed on one foot and a shoulder.

Pawan had broken his right collarbone. (This is only two years after my leg recovery.)

Eight days later, Nishant and I went skiing. It was absolutely gorgeous weather: Sun and bright blue skies, perfect snow, the weather only a few degrees below freezing. There were very few people on the slopes so no long lift lines. It doesn't get better than this for a skier!

As we were on our last run heading in, Nishant found a nice jump. But he didn't realize that behind that jump, another one had formed. He fell and was hurt. The ambulance took him to the hospital.

Nishant had broken his left collarbone.

Two brothers breaking the same bone essentially within a week?

What do you call that?

It's a bit difficult to get my head around addressing this challenge without being able to even name it.

SWITCH YOUR MINDSET:
A DIP IN A FROZEN LAKE

Two boys with broken collarbones make life a bit challenging.

Dressing has become a two-person job. Household chores are temporarily off the list. Temperaments are moody as Pawan and Nishant are restricted from contact sport for three months.

But there also is much they can do.

I walked into the kitchen the other day to see the boys working together to zipper up a jacket. (Priceless!)

Together, they can make a salad. The one who has a functioning left hand can hold vegetables while the other with the functioning right hand (they are both right-handed) can cut them.

The boys didn't want to hear my encouragement to look at what they can do. Perhaps this comes with age and maturity.

To switch their mindset, I took them for a dip in the frozen lake. Some people swear by it, others shake their heads in disbelief.

Being true to themselves, the boys bet on who could stay in the water the longest. When they could no longer feel their outer extremities, I ordered them out.

Now, I just have to convince them to join me on the mat.

— CHAPTER FIVE —

COPING

SMILE SIGNALS

Andreas, our oldest son, moved out last weekend to attend college in the Netherlands.

I told the remaining kids, "Good! Two down, two more to go!"

But that's only to hide how I really feel. I would like them all to stay home and close to me.

I am excited to see how happy Andreas is—he's already made friends and barely calls us. But I miss him. The house feels a bit empty. I cook less. There is less laundry. I receive fewer hugs.

It feels as if our part as parents is finished. I can only hope that we taught him well. I have to step back and simply revel in admiring my kids fly out and thrive as they mature, one by one.

In class, when a pose is hard, I sometimes advise my students to smile because it sends signals to the brain that the pose is not so difficult.

I am reminding myself to smile often these days.

LET BREATH BE FULL AGAIN

When we are sad, afraid, or stressed, we often round our upper backs to protect our internal organs. Our shoulders tense and our breath shallows.

This all leads to less than optimally functioning bodies. In return, that protected feeling, feeling better, isn't realized. Instead, open your heart and let the breath be full again.

JUST BE

Do you ever get sick the first days of your vacation? Or after a stressful time such as completing a large project?

It is not uncommon to get sick after a stressful period.

I was teaching a four-day retreat at the Juffing hotel that included a woman who had a migraine for two days.

I felt for her, as I also get frequent migraines.

The first day of the retreat she felt wonderful. Her neck pain had decreased, she felt happy and relaxed. The next two days she was in bed. But she was able to enjoy one last afternoon of the retreat.

Building time for relaxation every day can help prevent longer bouts of migraines and other headaches.

Fortunately, relaxation comes in so many forms. In Austria, I go for nature walks; in California, I walked on the beach; in Pennsylvania, I worked in the vegetable garden.

Relaxation also can take the form of meditation and mindfulness. Observe the scenery and the breeze on your skin. Watch the shifting of the water, the trees, ants building their anthill.

Take time to simply Be.

"Building time for relaxation every day can help prevent longer bouts of migraines and other headaches."

CHAPTER SIX

A TIME FOR ALL SEASONS

ALL THE SEASONS IN A DAY

Today we had snow, rain, and sunshine—real April weather.

It reminded me of California, where people often said that we experience all seasons in one day. We wore layers and kept extra sweaters in the car.

All the seasons in a day is like a yoga practice. I often feel so stiff and tight in the beginning, then I feel great and think I can go on forever, and suddenly I can't wait for Savasana.

Yoga is all things packed into one hour.

BREATH WORK OR ICE CREAM?

Summer is here.

Warm days remind me of a class I took at The Solebury Club in Bucks County, PA with colleague Maureen Shortt, who is an American Institute of Stress Fellow.

She introduced the class to a cooling breathing technique, Sitali Pranayama:

1. Curl the sides of your tongue to make the shape of a straw.

2. Breathe in, letting the air pass over your tongue. Feel the coolness on your tongue and in the back of your throat as air enters your mouth.

3. At the top of your inhale, press your tongue to the roof of the mouth as you seal your lips and hold your inhale for a moment.

4. Exhale completely through your nose.

After we did this breathwork for a while, Maureen smiled and told us that eating an ice cream also would work to cool us off!

WHEN IT RAINS, EAT KHICHURI

Fall is here.

The cows have come back down from the mountains, the kids are in school, and the weather has turned almost overnight from Summer to cold and rainy.

When it rains a lot in India, we eat Khichuri, a lentil and rice stew often served with fried slices of eggplant and an omelet.

Here is the recipe so you can also enjoy this simple, light and easily digested food during the rainy days.

KEEP MOVING IN DARKER DAYS

Winter has arrived in Tirol: We had our first snow today.

The boys and I went for a walk. The crispy sound of the snow under our feet made us nostalgic for younger-kid days in Pennsylvania when we'd sled, make snowmen, and host snowball fights; and of Sweden where we've always spent Christmas with family, interrupted only by the pandemic.

With shorter and colder days, I spend a lot more time indoors. I love to wrap myself in a blanket and watch a movie with the kids, or drink a cup of tea and chat with a friend.

But the lack of sunlight can make me feel tired, less energetic.

To combat that, I have a daily ritual: I light a candle, offer gratitude, and set an intention. Practicing yoga also often helps wipe the sluggishness out of my body and mind.

Whatever your fancy, keep moving in darker days.

Rainy Day Khichuri
Serves 4-6

INGREDIENTS:

3 dl (1¼ cups) yellow split peas, picked over, rinsed and drained
2 dl (¾ cup) basmati rice
60 ml (¼ cup) ghee, butter or canola oil
3 whole fried chilis
1½ teaspoon cumin seeds
2 bay leaves
8 whole cloves
4 black peppercorns
½ teaspoon turmeric
¼ teaspoon ground black pepper
2 medium onions, chopped
1.3 l (5¾ cups) water
1 ½ teaspoon salt, or to taste
¼ teaspoon garam masala

1. Combine the split peas and rice in a bowl and add cold water to cover; let soak for 20 minutes. Drain and set aside.
2. Combine ghee, butter or oil, the red chiles, cumin seeds, bay leaves, cloves, peppercorns, turmeric, and black pepper in a medium, heavy bottomed casserole over medium-high heat, cook, stirring for 2 minutes.
3. Add the onions and cook, stirring until they begin to wilt, about 3 minutes. Add the rice and split pea mixture and sauté, stirring gently so as not to break the rice, about 1 minute.
4. Add the water, salt, and garam masala and stir gently to mix.
5. Bring to a boil, turn the heat down to low, cover and simmer gently for 20 minutes. Stir gently. Then continue cooking, covered until the rice and lentils are tender and the mixture is still wet, like a very thick, savory porridge, about 5 more minutes. Taste for salt and serve hot.

Light some candles to celebrate the turn of the season.

SLURPEE SEASON

Today was my last ski day for this season. Lifts don't close until Easter, but the snow was so wet it felt like skiing through a 7-Eleven Slurpee®.

I came home and saw that crocuses were blooming and bushes budding.

Spring is definitely here!

Spring is the world coming alive again. People are out walking, riding bikes, and enjoying a beer in the yard. Kids play soccer in the fields and find fun things to do in the small creek behind our house.

People smile more during these first warm days.

While I am always a bit sad to stash away my skis for the season, I am happy to sit on the couch outside and watch the birds taking a bath in the pond.

"While I am always a bit sad to stash away my skis for the season, I am happy to sit on the couch outside and watch the birds taking a bath in the pond."

CHAPTER SEVEN

BE PRESENT

CHAT WITH THE HORSES

One of my favorite things about living in a small alpine village is to watch the local kids walk themselves to school.

The children chat, sing, and laugh. They walk in all weather: sun, rain, snow. The youngest ones cannot be more than four years old.

They don't seem to be in any rush to get to their destination. They stop to pet the horses. They pick up an interesting pebble. They watch bugs. They chat with a neighbor, pick flowers, or play a game along their way to school.

When I walk their route, I don't stop to chat with the horses. I have a goal in mind and want to get to my goal in the most direct way.

In our yoga practice, we sometimes focus on getting into a pose or to the final pose of a class, instead of enjoying the journey to attain it. We will get to a final pose, the class will end, no doubt about it.

I remind myself to learn from the school children, to enjoy the journey.

But enjoying the journey while cleaning bathrooms or grocery shopping is difficult!

What is more easily possible is enjoying the natural beauty on my drive to work, or being in the moment when I talk to a friend or cook dinner for my family.

"I remind myself to learn from the school children, to enjoy the journey."

FLEETING FRIENDS

I am still opening up and sorting through boxes in the basement from our move to Austria.

I found pictures from our years in Singapore in the early 2000s.

I have many fond memories of living in Singapore and have said that if the opportunity comes again, I would love to move back for a little while.

Singapore is at once both a place to return but a place many don't stay.

When we lived in Singapore, our social world was primarily other foreigners sent by American or European headquarters for a few years for a defined project. They established a factory, a research center, a sales department.

We knew when we met people for the first time that it would be a friendship of only a few months; at most, a few years.

But it was amazing how solid and important those fleeting friendships were.

We celebrated baptisms and a Brit Milah. We cared for each other's kids when someone was sick, shared intimate dinners on the beach, and always had an open door for anyone passing by to have a cup of tea or afternoon snack, or to share a coconut water on the beach.

Two months later, these wonderful friends would move to a new country or a new continent.

Our lives continually include these beautiful, short relationships. We become friends with other parents at school, colleagues at work, volunteers from a church event we all helped organized. When the kids move to different schools, new friends come and old ones fade.

Each and every friendship has taught me something.

I look forward to the time when a Singapore or other fleeting friend rings our doorbell so we can once again enjoy a cup of tea and reminisce about the beautiful times we shared.

Rocio's Authentic Mexican Guacamole for Snacking or Tacos
From a Mexican friend met in Singapore

INGREDIENTS:

4 medium tomatoes
4 avocados (make sure they are ripe)
1 small onion
1 small bunch of cilantro, chopped
2-3 green chilis (chili padi is OK)
Juice of half a green lemon
Tortilla chips (natural) for serving

1. *Cut tomatoes in half, remove seeds with a teaspoon, then chop flesh and put into a bowl.*
2. *Add a small onion, chopped very, very finely.*
3. *Add cilantro and chillies, also chopped finely.*
4. *Cut avocados in half, remove the pits, and scoop out the flesh. Place in a blender or mash manually, until almost smooth.*
5. *Stir in the lemon juice (very important step!).*
6. *Transfer into the bowl with the rest of the ingredients; add salt and pepper. Mix well.*

Enjoy immediately!

HOMETOWN BEAUTY

When you live in an attractive place such as our quaint village, friends and family visit often.

Recently, we had friends drop in who are biking from the Netherlands to Rome and back. Friends from Pennsylvania will visit soon, and we have family from California staying with us.

Naturally, we entertain our visitors by taking them out and about.

We show them the natural beauty of this place, visit historical sights, sightsee in nearby cities, and eat local food.

When we have guests, we also act like visitors. We enjoy a coffee or an ice cream in town, yet I don't seem to have time to enjoy our cute little plaza otherwise.

In the twenty years I lived in Pennsylvania through 2017, we visited the Philadelphia Museum of Art and Valley Forge, a major American historical sight, only a handful of times although both were less than an hour away from us. We visited New York City only annually when we could have caught the train for a day visit every weekend. Now that I live an ocean away, I regret not getting to know the area better.

The background of our hometowns become so much a part of us that we forget to take thirty minutes to enjoy a tea and people-watch at the town square.

Amid my daily routine, I am adding to my to-do list: Enjoying Local Beer in a Sunny Spot in Town or Visiting Nearby Museum About Invention of Sewing Machine. I have never visited the acclaimed gin bar in town nor hiked even half the trails in the area.

Local Kaiserschmarrn with Stewed Plums

Austrian dessert, but can be served as a lighter meal

INGREDIENTS:

4 eggs
2 tablespoons yoghurt
125 ml (½ cup) milk
2 tablespoons raisins
1 tablespoon granulated sugar
90 grams (3 oz) flour
30 grams (Almost 2 oz) butter or oil
1 teaspoon vanilla sugar
Salt
Icing sugar for dusting

1. *Preheat oven to 180°C (360°F)*
2. *Separate the eggs.*
3. *Mix the egg yolks, milk and yoghurt.*
4. *Whisk the egg whites with granulated sugar, vanilla sugar and salt until creamy and stiff, then fold into the batter.*
5. *Carefully stir in the flour, then add the raisins.*
6. *Heat the butter in an ovenproof pan, pour in the batter, and sprinkle with 1/2 tablespoon of granulated sugar.*
7. *Bake in the oven for about 20 minutes.*
8. *Tear the Kaiserschmarrn into pieces using two ovenproof forks.*
9. *Sprinkle with icing sugar before serving.*

Serve with stewed plums or apple sauce.

THE TREEHOUSE

Pawan and his friends have been building a treehouse in our yard.

He gathers tools, materials from the old kitchen that the carpenter has yet to get rid of, and friends to get the work done. They play the radio while they hammer, drill, and discuss next steps. Sometimes, the boys ask for advice or permission; but mostly, they ask for more snacks and supplies.

I love their enthusiasm. I admire their trying and failing and trying again, their improvisations, their energy, and their excitement Arindam and I don't help them. It's their design. If it works out, it's their success. If it falls apart, it's up to them to figure out what went wrong and how to fix it.

But I don't think they are thinking of the end result. I envy them.

CHAPTER EIGHT

EVERYWHERE IS GOOD

INDIA IS NEVER BORING

I read that one can only love or hate India.

I love India. And this week we are flying to visit family there. I cannot wait!

We haven't been to India in four years. I am looking forward to seeing my mother-in-law and so many other family members. I am looking forward to the food, the views, the shopping, and the smells.

It's never easy to witness the poverty and pollution. But there are people everywhere.

And you never know what you will encounter next: A cow in the middle of a busy roundabout, locals drying their rice on the highway, decorated trucks. I once saw a woman breastfeeding her infant on the back of a motorcycle while her husband swerved to avoid potholes and goats.

India is never boring.

BE MORE AMERICAN

This week, as I was teaching at the Juffing hotel where most guests are Germans, I began to wonder if I had lost my touch with people.

At the end of class, I included this beautiful, long Savasana in which I guided students through meditation. Everyone appeared comfortable with bolsters, blocks, and blankets supporting them. When it was time to get up, nobody wanted to move. Students walked out with that yoga-bliss look in their eyes.

As we were packing up, I made small-talk with some remaining students:

"You had a nice Savasana?"

One person half-grunted and another commented, "It was OK."

I was caught off-guard by the comments, but I shrugged it off. I cannot make people like Savasana.

The next day, both the grunter and the other person returned to class. When I asked if anyone had a wish or need, both of them asked for a long Savasana, "like yesterday."

I discussed this with a friend. She advised me that when a local declares something, "OK," or "Not bad," it means, "It's really good."

Dutch and Swedes also are understated. I grew up with understatement.

But we moved here from the United States, where Americans are demonstrative, even gushing. When I first moved to the United States from the Netherlands, I was overwhelmed by compliments.

After a yoga class, Americans would tell me they felt Wonderful! So relaxed! People had Fabulous days and the ice cream they ate was *to die for*. They had Incredible jobs.

I don't think American ice cream tastes better than European, and my guess is one person's *incredible* job is the same as another's *alright* job, depending on which side of the ocean they live.

I take the best of all cultures I have the good fortune to experience.

So, I am determined to be more American.

When it is dark and cold outside, a little extra positiveness can help lift spirits. I might give a cashier a compliment, have an incredible cup of coffee with a friend, or point out a student's Awesome pose!

PEDRO'S TACOS AND THE FLIXBUS

Yesterday was exactly four years ago that we arrived in Austria.

I remember it well. We had arrived late at night in the winter of 2020, and when we awoke the next morning, a Monday, we needed a few groceries.

We headed into the village but everything was closed with no signs on the door indicating the reason why. It was the same at the market, the bakery, and the butcher. It was Three Kings Day, only one of many Austrian holidays of which I was unaware.

We found food at the gas station in a larger nearby town. Our first meal in Austria was pasta with tomato sauce, cucumber, and a glass of red wine. We have celebrated this anniversary with our same gas station dinner ever since. (Also, I always have pasta and some tomato sauce at home.)

In the last four years, we have learned so much and gained so many new experiences with the help of friends. Our ever-patient German tutor sometimes met Pawan three times a week to prepare him for his German exam. We called on so many when we had questions about how to buy a bus ticket, or what the younger boys needed for school without an official Back-to-School shopping list as American schools provided.

I am quite often homesick for our lives in Pennsylvania and California. I miss large parking spots. I miss the ease of talking to people in the stores or on the street. I miss the positivity of Americans, whose first reaction to an idea is often, "Yes! Let's try it!"

I miss the ocean, surfing, and Pedro's tacos afterward. I miss our friends.

But I also really like our lives here.

The boys have so much freedom compared with the United States. They take the Flixbus to the Netherlands from about fifteen years of age. A couple of times when Pawan was ten, he called me from Innsbruck about an hour away: A few school friends took the train to have burgers there since they were better than the ones here.

I like to see how my brain has grown and learned a new language.

I enjoy the mountains and I love our new friends.

Arindam always says: "I am just so fortunate that I have been able to have gotten the opportunity and had the experience." He doesn't go around thinking what he is missing. He is just happy he can look back at so many wonderful adventures.

He is a wise man.

"In the last four years, we have learned so much and gained so many new experiences with the help of friends. I am quite homesick for our lives in the United States. But I also really like our lives here in Austria."

THANKSGIVING IN AUSTRIA

Thanksgiving is not a holiday I grew up with nor understood when I first arrived in the United States. But it is a holiday one learns quickly. The entire country shuts down and gets in Turkey Mood.

Three graduate students from India (my husband one of them) started celebrating Thanksgiving together when they arrived in the States in the 1990s. A few years later, wives joined the party, then not long after that, kids started arriving.

All our children are American, so we developed our own Thanksgiving traditions. We took turns hosting the same families for the whole weekend. The kids ran around all day outside, then slept soundly in piles at

Best American Thanksgiving Cranberry Sauce

INGREDIENTS:

125 ml (½ cup) fresh orange juice, from two oranges
125 ml (½ cup) cwater
180 ml (¾ cup) plus 2 tablespoons sugar
1 340 grams (12 oz) bag fresh or frozen cranberries
Zest of one orange, about 2 teaspoons
Pinch of salt

1. *In a medium sauce pan over high heat, bring the orange juice, water and sugar to a boil.*
2. *Add the cranberries, orange zest, and salt and return to a boil.*
3. *Reduce the heat to medium and boil gently for 10-12 minutes, until most of cranberries have burst open (you may need to mash them a bit with a spoon).*
4. *Transfer sauce to a serving bowl.*

Cover and chill until ready to serve.

night. The day after Thanksgiving, we went ice skating in Boston, or walked around Philadelphia's Reading Terminal Market, or explored Millenium Park in Chicago, or took a walk on the beach in California.

Thanksgiving turned from a festivity we didn't know how to celebrate into our most favorite holiday of the year. Our American friends teased that our Thanksgiving meal was more traditional than theirs.

Today, we are hosting a Thanksgiving dinner here with our Austrian friends. It's not on a Thursday, we have to work the next day, and I had to order the turkey in the summer (and pay three times the price for it) since turkey isn't a common meat here.

But we are all cooking together just as Thanksgiving entails. We have traditional sweet potatoes, cranberry sauce, stuffing, and brussel sprouts.

I am grateful for our new friends who are excited to learn about a new celebration. I am grateful for all the beautiful Thanksgiving memories from years past. And I am grateful for all who keep showing up on the mat with me.

LOVE BINDS US ALL

We spent a wonderful weekend in Lausanne, Switzerland, with my younger sister and her family.

We swam, went for a beautiful walk through the vineyards, visited the local farmers market, played games, ate great food and chatted for hours. It is my favorite way to spend a weekend with family.

At dinner outside in the yard one evening, we realized that we represented four continents, seven nationalities, eight languages (with English being the common one), and four religions.

Arindam and my Egyptian brother-in-law sought similarities between Indian and Egyptian cultures. We all enjoyed French cheeses and wines, even though France was represented by only one passport at the table. We poked fun of the "practical Lutheran" Swedish culture compared with the "stay in the moment" Eastern cultures. And across cultures, adults explained to the youngsters how hard it was Back in the Day.

The one thing that fused us: Love.

WHEREVER YOU ARE, TIME WITH GOOD-FEELS PEOPLE

We had a beautiful visit to Bucks County, PA with family and friends. We ate, laughed, did yoga, molded clay, then ate some more, talked, and hugged.

I lived almost twenty years in Pennsylvania, most of it in Bucks County, so it felt like coming home. I teared up upon landing at Newark (New Jersey) Airport, among the ugliest in the world.

I've only been back in Austria for a moment and I already miss my crazy, fun-loving, exciting, generous American friends.

But I also enjoy my fun-loving, German-speaking, exciting, and generous Austrian friends.

Wherever you are, spend time with those people who make you feel good, with those who make you happy, and with those who inspire you.

— CHAPTER NINE —

AGING

STUPID GLASSES

My optician advised that the cause of my migraines was an unevenness in my eyesight. The only way to correct this would be to wear glasses.

I don't like to wear glasses, but I don't like getting migraines even more.

And the glasses have worked. My migraine frequency is only once every few months instead once every ten days. What a relief! It has taken years to find a solution. From blood tests to MRIs to acupuncture to abstaining from wine, nothing previously worked.

But wearing glasses screws with my balance. That's a bit of an occupational challenge as a yoga instructor. Headstand and other poses where my eyes are closed work fine, but Tree Pose and other "easier" balance poses do not work well for me now.

Stupid glasses, I initially thought.

But now I view it as a challenge to overcome. Our bodies change due to age, injury or disease, changes in lifestyle, conditions such as pregnancy. There is no point in fighting it.

One way I am overcoming my balancing challenge is to replace frustration, my go-to reaction, with a smile when I fall out of and get back into a pose. Plus, I am adding a bit more practice.

Now when I fall, I talk to myself as I do with my students: "Nice try!! I like the effort and the smile! Let's do it again!"

"Now when I fall, I talk to myself as I do with my students: "Nice try!! I like the effort and the smile! Let's do it again!"

SHOWING UP IN NEW WAYS

As we age, we lose some skills, maintain status quo with others, and continue to work toward improving ones that have become increasingly important to us when the noise from the outside world about what should be important slips away and we listen to our hearts.

I don't even try to help our kids with math anymore. (This is Arindam's job.) And I don't need to be a better skier. I enjoy the exercise, the fresh air, and time with the boys on the chairlift. I enjoy them teasing me for being so slow that they have to wait at the bottom *for hours*.

But I like that my German is improving and that I am starting to understand and speak in local dialect.

And I like to keep my yoga practice at a high level, even advance it. I make a serious effort toward that. I practice regularly on my own and with other teachers, push myself when I would prefer to stay on the couch with a good book, and work to maintain a healthy lifestyle.

But also, I don't always need crazy poses such as headstand into Astavakrasana, (Eight-Angle pose, as I am here with my friend, Karin Eisen) that I sought when I began my yoga practice decades ago.

I find that a more gentle practice some days can give me as much joy.

My body has changed as I grow older.

But it is still this body that carries me through the day. I want to take care of it so it can carry me through many more days to come.

"My body has changed as I grow older. But it is still this body that carries me through the day."

MY EGO IS NOT SO HAPPY

I always thought (or wished) that I was indispensable at home. That without me, there would not be good food on the table, that dirty clothes would pile up, and that the house would be filthy.

But when I hobbled around with crutches all day and it was too difficult for me to run the house, I recognized my family is quite independent.

Pawan made wonderful nachos. Linnea made cheese fondue. Nishant made fish tacos. Andreas will be making a quinoa salad, and Arindam made lunches with potato curry. When we had guests, there were homemade chocolate chip cookies.

There were more dust bunnies, but nobody went without clean underwear. The bathrooms were not spotless, but they passed. The plants were watered, not wilted.

My ego is not so happy.

But then I realized, I am succeeding in a parent's job of teaching our children to be independent and self-sufficient.

I follow the same theory in yoga. I emphasize alignment and how to stay safe in a pose so that my students can be safe in any other live or online class they join. It empowers the student.

And that does make me happy!

"But then I realized, I am succeeding in a parent's job of teaching our children to be independent and self-sufficient."

Linnea's Swiss Cheese Fondue
Bonniers nya kokbok

INGREDIENTS:

500 grams (17½ oz) cheese (Emmentaler, gruyere)
1 small bottle of white wine
1 garlic clove
1 tablespoon potato flour or maizena
2-3 tablespoons kirsch (optional)
1 baguette

1. *Rub the inside of a fondue pot, or nice thick bottomed pot with the garlic clove.*
2. *Cut the cheese in small cubes add it to the fondue pan, add the wine and kirsch if using, let it melt on low heat on the stove.*
3. *Mix the maizena or potato flour with twice the amount of water; add this to the cheese mixture when it is melted. Let it start to bubble up, as soon as it boils turn down the heat. It should from now on only be kept warm, not boil.*

Dip small pieces of the bread into the hot melted cheese. Serve with a green salad and a glass of wine.

Boys' Chocolate Chip Cookies

INGREDIENTS:

190 grams (1½ cups) flour
1 teaspoon salt
¾ teaspoon baking powder
180 ml (¾ cup) butter
125 grams (1 cup) dark brown sugar
32 grams (¼ cup) granulated sugar
1 large egg
2 egg yolks
2 teaspoons vanilla extract
180 grams (6 oz) chocolate chips or cut up dark chocolate.

1. *Cook ½ cup of butter in a pot, making sure to stir often and scrape the bottom. The butter should brown, keep stirring. This takes about 4 minutes. Pour in a bowl and add the rest of the butter in small pieces.*
2. *When butter has melted, add the sugars and whisk well.*
3. *Add the egg and the egg yolks, plus the vanilla extract.*
4. *In separate bowl, mix the dry ingredients, then mix the wet ingredients to the dry. Carefully add the chocolate chips.*
5. *Use an ice cream scoop or large tablespoon to divide dough in about 16 balls onto baking paper*
6. *Bake at 190°C (375 °F) for about 8-10 minutes.*

Let cool and enjoy!

THE COMPANY WE KEEP

If the saying, "You are the company you keep" is true, then we regressed by a few decades this weekend!

We celebrated Andreas' twenty-first birthday yesterday with a barbeque in his honor. We spent the evening with him and his friends discussing their lives, joking, and having a good time.

The older boys don't plow through mounds of food as they used to, so we used leftovers today with a sweet couple we had met the first week we moved to Austria. They just celebrated their thirtieth birthdays.

If you do not hang out with a young crew regularly, inversions will keep you youthful!

WHAT IS OLD?

I was driving and listening with half an ear to the radio right up until the DJ asked listeners, "When are you old?"

This perked up my attention, especially when one listener defined old as fifty. I was shocked! According to this listener, I have been old for a few years.

I do not consider myself old, nor do I feel old.

In my mind, "old" means I have figured out life and I am content with all of it.

Yet some days I still wonder what I want to do when I grow up.

At dinner I asked my family the same "define old" question.

The boys answered that Arindam and I are old; we have always been old. Our childhood was at the time the dinosaurs still roamed Earth. (I wonder, then, what they call their great-grandmothers pictured here?)

Arindam said "old" is when there is not much hair to comb and when the body is still sore two days after playing basketball.

In yoga, we say that you are as old as your spine is flexible.

To stay young, bend and twist the spine in all directions.

Grandmother Dida's Egg Curry

INGREDIENTS:

4 eggs
4 small potatoes
1 tablespoon ginger paste
2 small purple onions
1 teaspoon chili powder
1 teaspoon turmeric powder
125 ml (½ cup) plain yoghurt or half tomato
1 bayleaf
1 teaspoon cumin
.2 inches cinnamon stick
4 cardamon seeds
2 cloves
2 tablespoons ghee or olive oil
Mustard oil (optional)

1. *Hard boil the eggs and cook potatoes till almost done.*
2. *Fry eggs and potatoes seasoned with half teaspoon turmeric and 1 teaspoon salt.*
3. *Remove from pan and set aside.*
4. *Add 1 tablespoon of ghee or olive oil to pan and fry the chopped onion till brown.*
5. *Add ginger and tomatoes or yoghurt. Fry till brown and a bit mushy.*
6. *Add chili, turmeric and salt.*
7. *Stir well and fry for about 2 minutes. Mixture should be like a paste, add water if needed.*
8. *Add potatoes and 1 cup of water; simmer until potatoes are soft.*
9. *Add eggs.*
10. *Grind in mortar and pestle the cinnamon stick, cardamon seeds and cloves.*
11. *In a clean frying pan, add 1 teaspoon of mustard oil, ghee or olive oil. When hot, add ½ teaspoon cumin, bayleaf and the ground cinnamon, cardamon and cloves.*
12. *Fry for about 1 minute; add the whole curry in this and let boil for another minute or so.*

Serve with rice.

A TASTE OF THE FUTURE

Arindam and I are getting a taste of what the future holds for us, and I am not sure I like it.

With four kids ranging in age from twenty-four years to fourteen years, our lives for a long time have revolved around them.

But they are getting older. Linnea, our oldest, and Andreas, our oldest son, live on their own in the Netherlands. Nishant lives at home but is off dog-sitting for a few days. Pawan, the youngest, took the Flixbus to Amsterdam today.

People always told me to enjoy the moment, the kids are big before you know it.

And I did enjoy the time when they were young. But also, it was hard! While there are some days I ache for the feel of rocking a baby in my arms to sleep just one more time, I also clearly recall that those sleepless nights seemed endless.

Yoga helps us lean into discomfort. Holding a pose as the mind starts to complain is, as some teachers say, the point when the pose starts. It's the point of growth.

Now I sit in a quiet house. I do not have to cook for an army nor do loads of laundry. It is unsettling. But I know that a new chapter will come soon, a chapter with new opportunities.

Until then, I will lean into the discomfort of being an empty-nester.

— CHAPTER TEN —

GROWING

DIVING IN

The owner of the Juffing hotel & spa where I am the main yoga teacher has a good business head. She wants to remain abreast of the latest guest experiences. The hotel offers yoga, aqua aerobics, Smovey workouts, Qi Gong, Wald Baden (forest bathing), hula hoop, and more.

Recently, the owner asked the entire spa team—yoga instructors and fitness trainers, massage therapists and beauticians— to learn more about aquatic fitness.

I was hesitant at the request. I didn't picture myself as an aqua fitness trainer. But I knew it would be a good skill to have if I needed to substitute for an aquatics instructor.

The training was actually much fun! We spent eight hours moving in the pool through cardiovascular workouts, balancing, strengthening, and relaxation. We pushed each other off our boards, held one-legged races across the pool, lifted bicep curls until our arms hurt, and finished with floating sessions.

We worked so hard that the side of the pool was flooded with water and the adjoining sauna had two inches of water on the floor.

In another month, the hotel owner wants us to train for water fascia release.

I was the first to sign up.

EVERYTHING IS POSSIBLE

This weekend, we tried water skiing.

I initially didn't want to go. I already broke one leg snow skiing; water skiing is for my next life.

But Pawan and his friend got up on their first tries, which encouraged me. The instructor explained what to do so clearly and calmly that I felt confident that not much could go wrong.

I eventually managed to stay up and it was enthralling to be pulled by such force! After a while, though, my legs tired, my thighs quivered, and my hips and butt burned. All I could do was hold on, keep going, and breathe.

Now my sister wants to try water skiing when she visits next week. I know I will join her.

But my hips and butt need to be stronger to not suffer the next day and have what Germans call Muskelkater, a muscle hangover. Utkatasanas (Chair Pose) and hip strengtheners, poses students do not love, will counterbalance that. But when I teach these, I will keep our water ski instructor in mind and use clear, slow instructions. We will hold the poses and just take one breath at a time.

Everything will be possible.

"German has the perfect word for being sore after a good workout: "Muskelkater." It translates to "muscle hangover," which describes that soreness better than any language I know."

SMILING HEART FACE

My kids accuse me of being a witch and I have finally proved them right.

I signed up with a friend for a workshop on harvesting edible tree buds. Tree buds, pollen, and small leaves have many beneficial nutrients. Black currant buds are said to be good against allergies and to improve the immune system. Other buds help with memory loss and inflammation reduction.

Now the kids will be eating a salad seasoned with birch tree buds to cleanse their blood and linden tree buds to strengthen their nerves.

The sweetest thing I learned was that when a leaf of a walnut tree falls off, it leaves behind a smiling heart face.

Denise's Bud Pesto
From owner of NaturVerbunden, a certified forest educator

INGREDIENTS:

1 handful of buds (Tree buds such as linden, poplar, maple, birch, walnut, beech; or fruit trees such as cherry, apple, plumb. Shrubs such as hazelnut, blackberry, raspberry or currant also are good.)
Nearly 159 grams (5 ½ oz) of almonds, pine nuts or sunflower seeds
½ teaspoon salt
a little more than 150 ml (½ cup) olive oil

1. *Put ingredients in a blender and blend till smooth.*
2. *If pesto is too dry, add more oil.*
3. *Put the pesto in small (glass) containers, then pour a little oil over it.*

Stays good in the refrigerator for about 6 weeks.

TWENTY-FIVE TEENAGE GIRLS

I was asked to teach yoga for Sports Day at the local school. I agreed, knowing but liking that it would be a challenge. I prefer to teach people in their Golden Years.

Details unfolded about the class as the day grew closer. Twenty-five—twenty-five! —girls ages twelve to fourteen signed up. The class was for two and a half hours.

What would I do with these kids for that long? But I could not, and did not want to, back out.

I looked at each point separately. The class could be broken down into four parts: Introduction to each other and to yoga, Asana practice, Relaxation, and Clean-up. Tweens and teens are not really children anymore so I can treat them more like adults willing to play.

This could be fun.

Then it dawned on me that I would have to teach the class in German.

I cannot be funny in German. I cannot express myself well yet.

I can say, "Oh wow, that's a nice pose." But I cannot say, "That looks gorgeous! Fabulous! Awesome!" I can say, "You can do it!" But I cannot say, "You are a rockstar! Girl power!"

All I could do was be well-prepared, show up, and do my best.

During the class introduction, I shared with the girls what I liked about yoga and that I was nervous that they wouldn't like the class and/or that they could not understand me.

They looked at each other and me and shared a knowing sweet smile as if to say, Been there.

It was one of the most rewarding classes I have ever taught.

I hope I get this opportunity again.

BREAKING THE ICE

For more than a year and half, we have been living in our picturesque Austrian alpine village.

The village has a church, a fire station, a restaurant, a small grocery store, a brewery, and a few small distilleries. There is a local elementary school housed in the same building as the library and the youth center. We have a bakery where the locals go for afternoon tea or beer.

There are roughly 2,000 residents, most of whom have been here for generations. They have family nearby and enough friends since childhood that they are not interested in making new friendships. A friend who has lived here for more than twenty years is still not considered a local.

As newcomers, it's been difficult to integrate. So to break the ice, we invited neighbors for an Indian dinner.

We're hoping to go beyond sharing homegrown vegetables and watching houses when one of us is away to sharing a proper visit.

Arindam has put on the lamb biryani since morning and I have vacuumed the house. Now we are preparing for the onslaught of Tyrolian and German. One of our neighbors speaks solid English, so she can translate, if need be.

I feel outside my comfort zone to entertain people with whom we've been friendly—but just that—for an evening.

But ultimately, we did have a good evening and now we are really good neighbors. Stepping outside my comfort zone let me step into more of our new rural life.

Arindam's Lamb Biryani

INGREDIENTS:

500 grams (1 lb) lamb fillet
0.5 liter (2 cups) basmati rice
7 cm (3 inch) piece of fresh ginger, peeled and cut into thin strips
3 cloves garlic minced
½ teaspoon coriander seeds
1 teaspoon turmeric or ½ teaspoon saffron threads
3 teaspoons Biryani masala (spice blend)
250 ml (1 cup) plain yoghurt
3 dl (1 cup) peas
Toppings: fried onion, minced nuts

1. *Cut fillet into cubes.*
2. *Add ginger, garlic, turmeric, biryani masala and salt to the yoghurt and mix well.*
3. *Marinate fillet in yoghurt mixture overnight.*
4. *Next day, cook rice according to packaging. Add peas to the rice for the last 5 minutes.*
5. *Cook the marinated lamb cubes in cooking oil. When done, add the rice. Mix well.*
6. *Top with fried onions and minced nuts.*

"Take a moment right now to reflect how far you have come. Be proud of all that you have accomplished."

ALL YOU HAVE ACCOMPLISHED

Nishant and I returned to the local phone store. The young man was the same salesperson who helped us acquire our first Austrian phone numbers four years ago in January 2020.

He put down his work, looked up, and said, "I just have to tell you, your German has improved so much since the first time you came in here. Really improved a lot!"

And Germans and Austrians are not known to be generous with compliments.

It's difficult to notice daily growth.

But think about how you have evolved over the last few years. Consider how normal remote work and workouts are to you today. Consider your more global orientation and new connections with people worldwide post-pandemic. Consider that you have learned at least one new thing: a new recipe, a new craft, a new language, a new hometown. Consider that you continue to learn, adapt, and grow.

Take a moment right now to reflect how far you have come. Be proud of all that you have accomplished.

FOR THE JOY OF IT

Two of the boys and I are on the train back to Kufstein after a beautiful vacation.

It was nice to get away, but I'm looking forward to seeing my students! I feel fortunate that I enjoy my work so much.

"What would you do if you never had to work again?" Arindam asked me years ago.

My answer back then was that I would still teach yoga.

I would give him the same answer today.

ACKNOWLEDGEMENTS

My yoga student and editor, Lisa Horst, saw something in my weekly writings. She is the vision, the brain, and the energy behind this book. Not in my wildest dreams had I imagined writing a book! What a gift this opportunity has been.

Thank you to my husband, Arindam, for eternal support, for deep conversations, and for patiently checking my weekly emails for grammar (and particularly, lack of comma errors).

I am grateful for our four children, Linnea, Andreas, Nishant and Pawan, who give us so much joy, and love. I love our dinner conversations that range from politics, women's rights and racism to teachers and funny events in school to illegal business proposals to teasing us for being old.

It is never boring with you all around! All of you, my children, have often been the inspiration for my thoughts and ponderings, some of which has resulted in this book. Thanks especially to Linnea and Andreas for always being the reliable "back-up email checkers."

I thank my parents for always believing in me and my siblings, and for encouraging us to keep learning. My dad told me once a long time ago to learn something new each day and I still apply that in my life. Writing this book taught me much. Britta, thank you for your advice on the title and your feedback and thoughts for the book along the way. It often gave clarity on European views that were hard for me to express.

A heartfelt thank you to my teachers and mentors worldwide who have generously shared their knowledge with me. Also, thank you to my employers who have seen my potential and believed in my contributions to the places I have worked.

Gratitude to graphic designer Angelique Carmello for your stunning book design and for how much better your work made mine (and under deadline, no less).

Of course my students are the core to my success as a yoga instructor. Some have come to class once and others in both the United States and Europe have attended every week for decades. It has always been a great honor to guide you on your yogic path. And as this book shows, my students are an inspiration on and off their mats!

I am grateful for the many friends we have. Some of you are mentioned here but all of you are equally important in my heart. You have given me so much love, joy and support along the way.

When you live far from family, you rely heavily on friends. They are the ones you call when the kids are sick, the ones with whom you celebrate anniversaries and holidays. Some friends were made at the soccer field, at school events, and kid playdates. Some friends were made in art and yoga studios all over the world.

Throughout my global life, old friends have faded and new ones have come in. But every one of you has made an impact on me, and therefore was directly or indirectly an inspiration reflected in this book.

ABOUT THE AUTHOR

Anna Folmer is a yoga teacher with 500+ hours of formal training. She also holds a MSc. in Environmental Economics and Extension Sciences.

Of all the amazing global opportunities she has been given, the one Anna is most grateful for is the opportunity to raise her four children with her husband of almost 30 years. She currently lives in a small alpine village in Austria.

You can find Anna at www.annafromsweden.com.